SHANACHIE TOUR

A LIBRARY ROAD TRIP ACROSS AMERICA

By **Erik Boekesteijn** and
Jaap van de Geer

Photography by
Geert van den Boogaard

 **Information Today, Inc.**
Medford, New Jersey

First printing, 2008

ShanachieTour: A Library Road Trip Across America

Publisher's Note: The author and publisher have taken care in preparation of this book and DVD but make no expressed or implied warranty of any kind and assume no responsibility for errors or omissions. No liability is assumed for incidental or consequential damages in connection with or arising out of the use of the information or programs contained herein.

Library of Congress Cataloging-in-Publication Data

Boekesteijn, Erik, 1962-
  ShanachieTour : a library road trip across America / Erik Boekesteijn and Jaap van de Geer ; photographs by Geert van den Boogaard.
     p. cm.
  ISBN 978-1-57387-360-4
  1. Boekesteijn, Erik, 1962---Travel--United States. 2. Geer, Jaap van de, 1973---Travel--United States. 3. Boogaard, Geert van den--Travel--United States. 4. Librarians--Travel--United States. 5. Dutch--Travel--United States. 6. Librarians--United States--Interviews. 7. Libraries--United States--Case studies. 8. Librarians--Attitudes. 9. Libraries--Aims and objectives. 10. Library science--Forecasting. I. Geer, Jaap van de, 1973-II. Boogaard, Geert van den. III. Title. IV. Title: Shanachie Tour.
  Z720.A46N4 2008
  027.073--dc22

                                                                    2008034238

Printed and bound in the United States of America.

President and CEO: Thomas H. Hogan, Sr.
Editor-in-Chief and Publisher: John B. Bryans
Managing Editor: Amy M. Reeve
Project Editor: Kathy Dempsey
VP Graphics and Production: M. Heide Dengler
Book & Cover Designer: Lisa M. Boccadutre

1. sen·na·chie [**sen**-*uh*-kee] *noun Chiefly Scot., Irish.*
   a professional storyteller of family genealogy, history, and legend.

   Also, shanachie [**shan**-*uh*-kee]

   (Source: dictionary.reference.com/browse/sennachie)

2. Shanachie (variant of Sennachie). In Ireland and the Scottish Highlands: One professionally occupied in the study and transmission of traditional history, genealogy, and legend.

   (Source: *Oxford English Dictionary*)

The Shanachies (L–R): Geert, Jaan, and Erik

CONTENTS

Dedication and Acknowledgments

In the name of Erik's father, C. P. Boekesteijn, a true poet and Shanachie, we would like to dedicate these stories to all Shanachies around the world who acknowledge the essence of libraries and librarians as keepers, tellers, and makers of stories for now and forever.

This book and DVD would not have been made if it were not for the inspiration, love, and help from our loved ones. They contributed more than they know. Thanks go to Lyan, Lora, Nicky, and Wil Boekesteijn, Pim, Marjolein, Eppo van Nispen tot Sevenaer, Nova and Sara, Hans and Akke van de Geer, Anne, Berend Bruins, Dick Kaser, Kathy Dempsey, Marydee Ojala, Francien van Bussel, Fred de Jong, Marian Koren, The Netherlands Public Library Association, ProBiblio, Edo Postma, Robin van Slierendregt, Procesbureau Bibliotheekvernieuwing, and all of our colleagues at DOK and all of the great librarians we met along the way. There are too many to name them all, but they know they are in the very heart of this story.

Special thanks go out to our dear friends Michael Stephens and Jenny Levine, who were at the very start of the Tour.

Foreword

SPIRIT OF THE SHANACHIES

The ShanachieTour—the actual tour, and this volume and DVD—is about spirit: the spirit of librarians and libraries, and the spirits of the three authors of the experience/book you now hold. They are the authors of the possible and the vivid.

What makes us see or feel something vividly? The deepest color of blue? The sweetest scent of a flower? The energetic sound of city traffic? The taste of the freshest tomato? The fullest heart? Vividness offers us a more intense and concentrated version of a feeling or experience. It is awake, bright, joyful, deep. How do we share vivid moments? How do we understand these small or grand moments?

We tell stories! It is through the natural gift of storytelling that we reveal to others our identities and our spirits. The stories people tell one another create community and develop understanding, and they surprise, amuse, or touch us in ways that only stories of a fellow human can. Stories generate understanding of the human spirit.

The ShanachieTour, born out of the imaginations of Erik Boekesteijn, Jaap van de Geer, and Geert van den Boogaard, did not simply appear out of a mist but was itself the product of telling stories around a table full of friends. As the assembled group talked, the imaginations of these three gentlemen jumped on an idea that seemed impossible. Too much fun, too crazy, too enjoyable, and *way* too extravagant to be something a group of library professionals could do!

But these men are so infused with a spirit of openness and able-ness that the idea for a tour across the U.S. in a camper van by three Dutchmen from a small public library in the Netherlands did not seem outside the realm of the possible for them. Around the table that evening, they promised their American friends that they would secure not only the funding but also the "permission" to make this extraordinary story-collecting voyage across the U.S.

And within a matter of months, they sent word that they were on their way to the U.S. to do just as they had described at the party table: to drive around the country, visiting libraries and librarians, talking to people and recording these conversations and visits—collecting stories, being Shanachies, like the roving Irish storytellers of old.

What is the importance of this 3-week expedition? Just as early explorers roamed this country looking for settling places or good fortune, Erik, Jaap, and Geert—armed with laptops, cameras, video cameras, and sound equipment— roamed around a foreign place in a large mobile home (which they dubbed the MotherShip) looking for and collecting good stories. And yet the importance of this project goes beyond these facts.

I believe the importance of the ShanachieTour lies in the indomitable spirit and delight with which Erik, Jaap, and Geert went after and captured stories both grand and small. A good idea, a human idea, a seeking of understanding and connection are all at the heart of this unique experience. And the uniqueness of the experience was not just theirs but all of ours—all of us who were touched by or interviewed by or who dined with these roving story capturers, as I did.

Our own identities in U.S. libraries were made clearer to us through the stories we told them and through their engagement of those stories and their unique abilities to synthesize these into short but fun and spirited video casts.

The talents and charm of these three men (technical abilities, knowledge of libraries, and humor) are obvious, but the most extraordinary gift they each have is a conviction that all is possible!

- It is possible to raise money to travel 4,000 miles from home to capture library stories.

- It is possible to spend 3 weeks away from home and work.

- It is possible to convince your boss to let you run around the U.S.

- It is possible for small public library employees to talk on a level playing field with senior leaders of large research libraries.

- It is possible to overcome illness and exhaustion to gather even more stories.

- It is possible to cook amazing meals and upload podcasts and music in the evening light of the wilderness areas of the U.S.

- It is possible to create a more global sense of what a library is and what is important about libraries through stories.

- It is possible to energize people you don't even know through your enthusiasm and irrepressible joy.

- It is possible to make this tour an ongoing project in other places. (Just watch them!)

It is possible. It is fun. It is about making the community of libraries more obvious to itself. Through this all-too-brief tour, we learned about ourselves through them. Erik, Jaap, and Geert have graced the U.S. with such a spirit of possibility, and have shone brilliant sunlight on us and our community. Now it reflects back on them as we embrace them and their project of being Shanachies for all of us.

Now, turn the page and relive their tour through this wonderful volume and DVD.

Kathryn J. Deiss
Content Strategist
Association of College & Research Libraries,
a division of the American Library Association
Chicago, IL

Editor's Preface

When three Dutchmen visited Chicago to film a library documentary in early 2007, they came up with the idea of returning that autumn for a full cross-country tour of U.S. libraries. Actually making that second trip seemed improbable at best. Yet they did it, and it was a totally original, groundbreaking adventure.

When these same men started dreaming about creating a book and a film detailing that U.S. "ShanachieTour," they faced many hurdles. The first publisher they approached turned them down. Since I had become a friend and believer in their cause, they came to me with some basic questions about publishing in the spring of 2008. I started helping them by gathering some info and making some phone calls to U.S. companies. As weeks went by, I became as determined as they were to make sure their story would be told, because it's an amazing promotional tool for libraries. Still, for various reasons, the book/movie project looked pretty improbable, too. But with a lot of persistence and a little luck, we found a publisher, and I was able to keep working with my colleagues as the book's editor.

In the months since then, this unique undertaking has been many things: frustrating (seeking music rights), complicated (the DVD aspect), tiring (communicating with folks in time zones from Europe to California), and tedious (keeping track of all the pieces). But it's also been *refreshing*. What's been so helpful to me, personally and professionally, is getting a new view of librarians' strengths, determination, and achievements.

I've been monitoring library technology, marketing, and promotion for more than a decade, and in that time I've grown tired. I've watched info pros of all types work incredibly hard to serve their customers. I've watched them toil through building initial websites, only to have people demand that more and more new features be added. I've watched them increase the number and scope of their community programs, only to be asked for even more. I've watched them fight battles for funding, only to be voted down too often by people who don't understand what a great library could really do for them.

Librarians reach out on so many levels, and although there are some wonderful successes, it seems that there are never enough. As technology changes at the speed of light and as other businesses encroach more and more on services that libraries have traditionally offered, I've sometimes felt like "We'll just never win." In the words of the band U2, it seems like a lot of hard-working librarians are just "running to stand still."

But now the spirit of the Shanachies has worn off on me. Even after 4 years as a paraprofessional and 15 more as an industry editor and speaker, suddenly I'm feeling more hopeful and less beaten down. I think that this book and movie will do the same for others in this fast-paced, constantly challenging field. That's why I wanted to help Erik, Jaap, and Geert carry their message and their energy to more of the world. That's why I've worked with them for many months to make their vision a reality.

I believe that everyone who reads this book and watches this film can also be imbued with the Shanachies' can-do attitude and their adventurous spirit. They've already accomplished things that many would have given up on. So why can't the rest of us?

Enjoy the journey and let the Shanachies' "anything is possible" mantra wash over you and rejuvenate your professional goals and dreams.

Kathy Dempsey
Editor, *Marketing Library Services*
and consultant, Libraries Are Essential
Medford, New Jersey

The Shanachies'
Cross-Country Trek

Erik on the plane to New York

CHAPTER

1

WEBLOG SHANACHIETOUR

*The Netherlands
to the U.S.A.
October 13, 2007
First 6,000 KM traveled*

Flying to New York

Finally it has really begun now. Left Schiphol Amsterdam and, on a big blue bird, we are flying to America. Lost Jaap and Geert in a totally absorbing *Die Hard* movie, as it seems. After some indefinable airbus food I long for good spicy New York food.

Not a clue how long it is going to take us to get through customs and to the hotel, but we will have to check the equipment as the last recordings had sound problems. We will grab a cab to Madison Square Garden to see Queens of the Stone Age. If there is any energy left after the concert and that midnight snack, we will probably finish Geert's assumed private bottle of expensive malt scotch.

Tomorrow we will hopefully have a beautiful morning in New York, do some street interviews and shoot some nice shots in Manhattan, after which we head out to meet and eat with John Blyberg and his family. Cannot wait to see that man. The story has begun and will unroll itself in the next 3 weeks. I expect nothing but thrills, pushing us to the very limits of our librarians' imaginations.

New York City scene

The Chrysler Building

Dinner with
John '3.0'
Blyberg

CHAPTER
2

WEBLOG SHANACHIETOUR

New York City and
Trumbull, Connecticut
October 14, 2007
6,240 KM traveled

OK. After 2 hours of trying to get our sound system to work and having warm feelings about the person who bought this garbage, we head out for Chinatown to get a proper meal. And a proper meal we did find. The Peking Duck House is confirmed to be the place to get Chinese food in New York. By the time we finished our dessert there was, for Jaap and

me, no energy left to make it to Madison Square Garden, but Geert is unstoppable when it comes to live music, so he went on his own. Jaap and I walked back to the hotel and fell in love with New York.

This love was only to grow the next morning. Lovely sunny weather on the ferry to Staten Island and back helped us to be firm and defy the guards on the ferry, who wanted us to stop filming. After the ferry we had to make one dream come true. The Apple Store on Fifth Avenue is a magnet to Apple addicts and I had to drag Jaap and Geert out of the overcrowded shop. Though not before buying that iPhone, iPod, and other gear. I'm sure I could hear my Shanachie credit card weep when we left the building.

After that it was time to make it to our dinner date with John Blyberg and his family in Trumbull, Connecticut. His wife had made an excellent dinner with an amazing tasting salmon. It is always special to meet someone in a home environment. John has only recently begun in Darien

*Geert and the filming equipment are all set to record
a segment outside the Apple Store in New York City.*

We passed the train station for Darien, where John Blyberg now works, on our way to his home in Trumbull,

Library, but he is full of ideas and a very bright man, so I am sure he will lift the library in the Darien community to a higher level. Cannot wait to see him again in Monterey.

But first there is New York Public and another inspiring man, Paul Holdengräber. From what I read he may be one of the highlights of the ShanachieTour. Guys let's put away that bottle and get some sleep. We have to rise with the sun in order to shine some light on the future of libraries. Even Shanachies need to sleep sometimes.

REARVIEW MIRROR REFLECTIONS: LEARNING FROM JOHN IN TRUMBULL

It was dark when we stopped at the station where we were supposed to meet John Blyberg. On our route from New York to Trumbull, we already passed Darien, where John has been working at the public library several months.

Everyone who wants to learn more about Library 2.0 or Web 2.0 sooner or later comes across one of John's projects. SOPAC, or Social OPAC, may very well be one of the most extraordinary undertakings so far. John built this SOPAC with the knowledge he acquired working in the IT department of the library of Ann Arbor. It was one of the first attempts to add Web 2.0 elements to a traditional (web) catalogue, thus creating the possibility for the user to add comments to titles within the catalogue. Besides this he developed a website based on the open source content management system DRUPAL that allowed users to give feedback and exchange information among themselves and librarians. The first online library

The first online library community website, AADL 3.0 [Ann Arbor District Library], much to the surprise of friend and foe, aroused an enormous interest from users and librarians. It was way beyond anyone's expectation.

community website, AADL 3.0 [Ann Arbor District Library], much to the surprise of friend and foe, aroused an enormous interest from users and librarians. It was way beyond anyone's expectation. In the first 2 months after the site was launched about 25,000 people joined and made accounts. This groundbreaking work gave John well-deserved recognition. He was elected Library Innovator of the Year and was offered a great job at Darien Library [www.darienlibrary.org] to weave his magic once again.

When we arrived at his beautiful house bordering a forest, we received a warm welcome by his wife and three children. After a dinner of wild salmon and fresh asparagus, we got to record a half-hour interview. On the question of whether the building of a website was a big investment, John answered that the first things needed to do the job were dedication and support by staff and board of directors. Once you have that, a similar website can be made within 6 months.

JOHN BLYBERG'S COMMENTARY

The Shanachies are storytellers in the truest sense of the word. By traveling across the country, they have paid homage to one of the world's most venerated professions by allowing the story of the American library to tell itself in the many voices and faces of the people they visited on their way from one ocean to another.

There was a wonderful metaphor in the Shanachie's westward trek. Following in the tradition of the Beats, the three of them headed west across the country with a camper, a video camera, and a guitar. Their sole purpose was to find and talk to librarians who were giving it their

all. One visit showed us the high-vaulted ele-
gance of the human mind, another brought
forth a story of persistence and humor in the
face of hard-scrabble librarianship. We saw
how one visionary was leading his students into
a new era of information science. We were
shown great technology and engaging spaces.
And one young tour guide in Salt Lake City
reminded us that the American Library is where
we go to "practice democracy."

But the real significance of the Shanachie-
Tour was not that it culminated in a wonderfully
encouraging and entertaining presentation and
an equally rousing documentary. The magic
was in the journey itself. Erik, Jaap, and Geert

John Blyberg at home

showed us that yes, we can still head West. The 21st-century library
remains largely undesigned. The information landscape is new and un-
charted, our relationship with it is untested, and the future is unknown.

Today's librarians are pioneers just as, in one way or another, everyone the Shanachies talked to are pioneers. And the Shanachies are themselves explorers whose message is as timely as it is imperative.

In visiting America, the Shanachies made it clear that their creativity and passion for libraries cannot be contained by national borders nor inhibited by any ocean. Their message and enthusiasm presages a new kind of library where humanity is encouraged.

John Blyberg
Head, Technology & Digital Initiatives
Darien Library
Darien, CT

Seeing the steps and the lions (Patience and Fortitude) of the New York Public Library left us speechless.

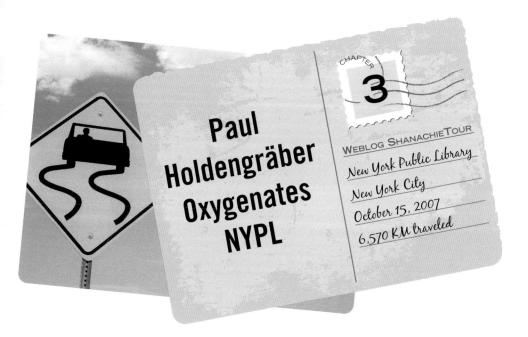

Paul
Holdengräber
Oxygenates
NYPL

CHAPTER

3

WEBLOG SHANACHIETOUR

New York Public Library

New York City

October 15, 2007

6,570 KM traveled

After a night in a stuffy hotel room without oxygen, which actually made Jaap wake up in the middle of the night screaming for air, we got out of our hotel at 8AM to meet Paul Holdengräber at The New York Public Library. Expectations were high as we knew the man was becoming well-known in New York for bringing great evening programs

Erik and Geert signing the contract to rent the MotherShip.

with debates on hot and interesting issues. These events are bringing more than 1,000 people to the library and only 25% are frequent visitors. No wonder, when you book Bill Clinton and Martin Scorsese.

When an old man dies, a library disappears.
—*Paul Holdengräber*

If it was not the library that kept us spellbound, it would have been Paul. What passion, what energy, what great intelligence and hunger for knowledge. I've rarely met a man who made such a first impression.

Talking about stories and Shanachies, he came up with the wonderful quotation: "When an old man dies, a library disappears." (That one is for you, Dad.) I think we got almost an hour of great material, which will definitely go online someday.

Away from the marble floors and the old wooden desks, we hit New York concrete only to get our luggage from the hotel and to take the train to New Jersey to get our camper. Then it will be off to Baltimore and Charlotte to meet the great Matt Gullett and see his beloved library. Tonight we will camp and cook steaks in our little kitchen. Miss my daughters back home, but the road is calling and we have a long way to go. North Virginia leaves turn in all colors and melancholy fills the air.

I simply love fall; it's my favorite season. Joni [Mitchell] is singing in my head: "Prisoners of the white lines of the freeway ..."

REARVIEW MIRROR REFLECTIONS:
THE UNIVERSE IS MADE OF STORIES

Our journey began in Manhattan, where a long-treasured dream came true—a visit to The New York Public Library [www.nypl.org], the biggest marble building in America (that is, when it was built in 1911). We were here in the first place to meet Paul Holdengräber, the man who is responsible for the Live Events in the massive library. With about 90 events a year, each attended by an average of 1,000 people, we can safely say he is doing an amazing publicity job. Paul has set himself the task of making the two lions at the building's entrance, Patience and Fortitude, roar. He also wants to make the library "levitate" and to make it the center of the society.

In spite of the fact that the building itself makes an enormous impression and plays an important part in the daily service, the library pays a lot of attention to digital developments. Paul himself will not easily use terms such as Web 2.0, but he makes sure that the NYPL is clearly visible and traceable on the web. For instance, all the events of "LIVE From The NYPL" are recorded and available via streaming on the website. Unfortunately the format that is used is Windows Media Video, which makes it only available for the Windows Media Player. Still it is a step in the right direction. It is good fun to watch old episodes with, for instance, [chef] Anthony Bourdain.

Both in the Netherlands and in the U.S.A., video is not used to a great extent, although there is such a great opportunity and a treasure of possible material. Imagine what sort of database we could create if we, that is all the libraries in the U.S.A. or even the world, recorded all events and made them available for the customers. This way, like the idea of the ShanachieTour, we can offer a whole new way to share stories. Not a bad idea during a time in which we have to fight for digital rights and the availability of affordable, high-quality, unique, work-related content.

While we were doing the interview with Paul in the astonishingly beautiful Reading Room, I remembered a blog I posted on one of the first Dutch library weblogs, OBlog. It dates back from December 9, 2004 and was about the start of lending ebooks in the NYPL through its website. Now it has a collection of thousands of digital books as well as a special

collection of ebooks for e-kids—animated books read out loud. All available for free online. Besides all this, MyLibraryDV offers the opportunity to download about a thousand movies and TV series for free. To combine all these services in one all-inclusive database is only a matter of time.

The fact that they take the digital library seriously in New York appears from the Media Lab they made available on the site. This lab gives a clear insight into what they call the digital experience. Here they experiment with weblogs about gaming or cooking, and discuss the search for ways to integrate social software in the services provided.

After the interview, the three of us just could not stop talking about Paul and his enthusiasm and vision and his belief in the power of the story and the eroticism of thinking. Then outside, we stumbled upon a tile in the concrete with this line: "The universe is made of stories, not of atoms." Wow, this is beautiful, but how do we as librarians meet with the challenges of this century? How can we remain that place where people come

NYPL's Main Reading Room

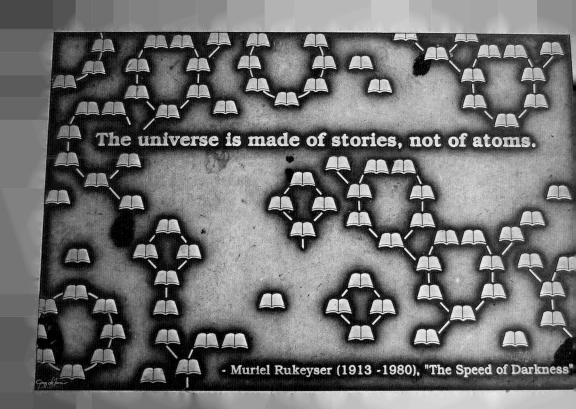

The universe is made of stories, not of atoms.

— Muriel Rukeyser (1913 -1980), "The Speed of Darkness"

to for their stories and information? With all the possibilities on the internet, how can we meet with the higher demands of the new generations?

In order to find answers, we Shanachies yet had a long way to go. The tour had really begun.

PAUL HOLDENGRÄBER'S COMMENTARY

What does it mean to be working for an institution, a major library, in my case The New York Public Library, which could become irrelevant, superfluous? With what some see as the onslaught of the internet, a life lived amongst the electronic mob, what is the place of the library? Freud wondered What Do Women Want, we might ask ourselves What Do Libraries Want. What can they deliver and what does the public need and seek? Here is a partial view. Thanks to a fabulous mistranslation into English of Andre Malraux's book *Le Musee Imaginaire* as *The Museum Without Walls*, we have a clue: Our new tools for research have brought us The Library Without Walls where we can access information from everywhere and anywhere without moving from our chair. Great!

Yet, we need places to meet. Spaces to think together. Libraries have in part become such charged gathering places, inviting writers and artists, politicians and chefs, filmmakers and philosophers to discuss and debate ideas, bringing to life the books on the shelves, but more than that making the life of the mind exciting again, compelling.

What we read can transform us. What we hear does as well. The ear is a very sensitive organ. Isabel Allende once said on our stage that in Latin America people talk about making love through the ear. The power of words. The library is a place for active listening. As much as the internet delivers a lot, it does not replace the attention of being together in a room listening to and participating in a lively talk, a conversation. We need to be together with others. We can't tickle ourselves. Try—it won't work. The trick it to make what is happening on stage exciting, sexy, alive. In two words: Cognitive Theater.

Paul Holdengräber
Director of Public Programs, "LIVE From The NYPL"
The New York Public Library
New York, NY

Erik with Paul Holdengräber at the
beginning of their interview in the NYPL

Matt Gullett Is Lifting Library Standards in Charlotte

CHAPTER

4

WEBLOG SHANACHIETOUR

Public Library of Charlotte
& Mecklenburg County
Charlotte, North Carolina

October 17, 2007

7,400 KM traveled

Very close to being arrested for illegal camping, we were, almost at gunpoint, directed to a spot in one of the darkest places I had ever seen. Exhausted as we were, we went to sleep early to wake up in a beautiful forest surrounded by squirrels and deer. The only thing missing was a white-faced girl with vivid red lips and a bundle of singing dwarves.

Inside ImaginOn, the youth center in the Public Library of Charlotte & Mecklenburg County

This fairytale kept us spellbound just a little too long, so we arrived late at Charlotte Mecklenburg Public Library. Luckily there was a parking place for our little home. Matt Gullett and comrades turned out to be exactly what we hoped for. Inspiring, innovative librarians, focusing on the future with the sense to measure the results of their innovations. Imagine game labs, music studios, animation studios, theatres, story-making rooms, computers that translate to Braille, computers for people with a handicap, you name it they have it in Charlotte. And like I said they measure the results of what they are doing and find that book circulation is increasing and that they are having more visitors every year, especially teens. The awareness of the new ways of making and telling stories is obviously present in Charlotte. Best practice for sure. Hope to be back in a couple of years, but we will definitely stay in touch. Thanks Matt, hope to see you in Monterey.

REARVIEW MIRROR REFLECTIONS:
THE YOUTH DEPARTMENT OF OUR DREAMS

In order to visit this library we had to get off our route west and go south via Washington DC to Virginia and drive an extra 650 miles. But after

The ImaginOn entrance

reading about the Public Library of Charlotte & Mecklenburg County [www.plcmc.org] and the unique co-operation with the children's theater, which lead to the building and opening of a special youth section called ImaginOn with a mission to bring stories to life, we were on our way.

And when Matt showed us the ins and outs of his dream library, it turned out to be worth every single extra mile. First thing Matt and his colleagues were eager to show us was the Gamelab, where a mobile game set-up can be moved to all libraries in the area with a program that is specially made to appeal to the adults as well as the kids.

Matt Gullett has an outspoken opinion on the importance of the digital library. Books are merely containers for information or fiction, just like the computers or film and discs. Depending on what we want to communicate in the future, there will be different demands on the containers. Matt believes that the book will remain a very good container for the novel and other fiction works, but for information, the internet may be easier. He sees a change or transformation from library to community learning center. In order to make this transformation it is essential to know all there is to know about the digital domain. We must be able to help our customers with all available digital sources and equipment such as ereaders, computer programs, and phones that can and will be used to keep, tell, and make stories.

We must be able to help our customers with all available digital sources and equipment such as ereaders, computer programs, and phones that can and will be used to keep, tell, and make stories.

Well, in Charlotte, this is well taken care of. The first person Matt introduced us to was Helene Blowers, who is working in Columbus now. She developed the so-called 23 Things program, a course that teaches people how to use the possibilities of Web 2.0 in 23 steps. Part of this course is how to make your own wiki or blog.

MATT GULLETT'S COMMENTARY

Stories are our lives. We have the stories of our birth, families, anniversaries, experiences, education, and so much more. Those stories intersect, consume, reflect, and run alongside the many stories that we read about in books, watch in films, interact with in games, and so on. Libraries have always been a community collector and facilitator of these life stories. People have always come to us to enhance and build their own stories through learning and entertaining.

Erik with Matt Gullett

As community centers that facilitate and collect stories, we are beginning to see the emergence of a new generation that has a real passion to not only passively intersect with the library in their story building, but they also desire more than ever to be an integral part of creating their own story within the context of the library and community. With such a desire upon our community cultures, we have an opportunity to meet their interest with many of the social software tools, the creative expression software, and technology that is available. More importantly, we can seize this opportunity to shift the mind-set of librarians to being more of an agent of active community change.

Matt Gullett
Emerging Technology Manager
Public Library of Charlotte & Mecklenburg County
Charlotte, NC

[Note: Matt has since moved and is now Lead Consultant,
Learning Experiences Group, Seattle, WA]

Sculpture outside
Charlotte's library

CHAPTER

5

WEBLOG SHANACHIE TOUR

Ann Arbor
District Library
Ann Arbor, Michigan
October 19, 2007
8,500 KM traveled

Eli Neiburger Puts G-Force in Ann Arbor's District Library

However ambitious we may be, the distance to Ann Arbor is not something we can do in 1 day. So from Charlotte we head out for a 5-hour drive in the Appalachian Mountains. Full of inspiration after our meeting with Matt [Gullett], we rolled through the red, brown, and green mountains in the late afternoon Indian summer sunset. Eventually we ended in coal-mining country, where the standards of living are at rock bottom. We actually saw this stereotype picture of a man sitting on his porch with a gun, but Geert, our hero, did not dare to ask if he could take his picture. Hmmm wonder why.

After a good night rest we set out for Buckeye Lake near Columbus, Ohio. Great thing about these campsites is that the one Shanachie without an Apple PowerBook still had excellent internet connection. haha. Didn't need your fancy Apples. (No, just kidding guys.) So we were able to put up new posts and video material. Did not feel very well so I went to bed early again, to wake up in an enormous thunderstorm that completely soaked our almost-dry laundry. From Ohio to Ann Arbor, Michigan is a 4-hour drive on which we discussed the wonderful things we heard about the place. Eli Neiburger is well-known as librarian and gamer and his gaming program takes him all over the country and even beyond the borders.

We wondered, on a large scale with many gaming events, would not the kids lose interest in time when the novelty wears off? No it definitely does not, says Eli. The scale is getting bigger and bigger and the

Kids competing at Dance Dance Revolution

software actually enables libraries now to keep scores and play against one another. This could even be done internationally so I think Delft will have to come up with an expert group of gamers, as what I have seen blows your mind. Impossible speed on the dance mats. Not in a thousand years could we Shanachies learn that. Eli is I think one the best-known persons in the community and popular among the kids and that is no wonder. What a man. So good to meet you and I know we will meet again soon. GAME ON Captain, the MotherShip says hi.

REARVIEW MIRROR REFLECTIONS: GAMES ARE A POWERFUL DRAW

After a stormy night with thunder and lightning in an RV park along the highway, we continued our way to Ann Arbor. A sort of bacteria had taken over and while my face turned green and hours were spent in the tiny bathroom, the MotherShip shook and bounced on and on in order to make it to our next appointment.

Ann Arbor District Library [www.aadl.org] and Eli Neiburger are known throughout the U.S.A. for their best practices on IT and gaming. It was a shock to find out that a library the size of DOK [our library in the Netherlands] employs 10 people in the IT department. Wow, what luxury and how does that pay off.

We were so lucky. That evening they were holding a Game Party. This happens frequently during tournament season, and it draws in an average of 80 teens from 10 to 18, but there are also evenings for the younger and older people. We saw boys and girls playing together on the Wii, the PlayStations, and the computer games. There were DDR, Guitar Hero, Wii Sports.

That these games are teaching these kids all sorts of skills is obvious, but Eli does not stop there. In a separate room there was a fully equipped studio, where the gamers can be filmed and give live comments on what happens in the game room. This is broadcast by the local television station. All organized and done by the kids themselves. Amazing.

Eli Neiburger is surrounded by technology in his gaming lab.

There in the IT department they were working on software that enables them to hold game events against other libraries across the U.S.A. and even against us in the Netherlands. Imagine kids in Delft playing against the kids in Ann Arbor. ... I guess we must practice soon, as these kids are way ahead of us.

Eli was very outspoken on a number of arguments on gaming in libraries. He said, "Whether it does increase the book circulation is irrelevant as we don't measure that after a reading session, so why after a game night?" He also said that gaming has proven to be the best way to bring in all age groups and have them play together in the library. That gaming makes the kids more aggressive is, in his opinion, absolutely not true. When he was young, he told us, kids used to beat each other up after school; now they fight one another in a game instead. When Eli shows us out, kids scream his name in the streets. They all seem to know him by name. This is best practice indeed. Web 2.0 in real life.

Whether it does increase the book circulation is irrelevant as we don't measure that after a reading session, so why after a game night?

—Eli Neiburger

ELI NEIBURGER'S COMMENTARY

The text from an exotic phone number was our first signal that the MotherShip was approaching. Before long, she appeared, looming over the horizon like a flying Winnebago, winding its way through Ann Arbor's maze of one-way streets until finally coming to rest across three spots in our staff lot. The MotherShip had landed. Shortly it vomited forth three Dutchmen, draped with Crumpler bags and boom mics, headphones and PowerBooks; a mobile storytelling unit ready to learn and share with the world.

Their time in Ann Arbor was all too brief; but somehow they squeezed a lot into 4 hours: a piercing and jovial interview in my office (stumping me with "What else do you like to do besides play videogames?"), a tour of the geeky refuges of our building, a visit to a DDR tournament, a failed attempt by Geert to defeat me on the dance pads, the eurofuelled purchase of an acoustic guitar on sale, and much laughing and drinking of coffee. Before we knew what had hit us, they were off again to Chicago and the promise of a berth for the MotherShip on the Dominican Campus.

A few days later, the video story of their visit to AADL emerged, and I was blown away by the sophistication of their presentation, from the titles to the music to the editing. These guys had production in their blood, and the way that they tell stories is an inspiration to libraries everywhere. Would that our own productions could be so polished, so informative, so light-hearted, and so freely given to all who are interested. We all need to become Shanachies, collecting and spreading knowledge and laughter around the world, and Erik, Jaap, and Geert have shown us how it should be done.

Eli Neiburger
Associate Director for IT and Product Development
Ann Arbor District Library
Ann Arbor, MI

Erik and Geert hanging out with the MotherShip,
which carried a banner with the logo of DOK,
the library they work for in Delft, the Netherlands.

Driving into Chicago

MotherShip
Touches
Home Base in
Chicago as We
Visit Michael
Stephens

CHAPTER

6

WEBLOG SHANACHIETOUR

Dominican University

River Forest, Illinois

October 20, 2007

9,100 KM traveled

After what I hope will be the worst drive of my life, we reached Chicago. My food poison reached its worst stage and I had to spend nearly 4 hours of the night trip to Chicago banging against bathroom walls trying to sit on the toilet. My prayers were heard and we did reach Dominican University alive, where friendly security allowed us to

stay overnight on campus. First thing in the morning, I was calling Michael Stephens to please come to the rescue with some proper medicine, which he did and which made it possible for me to get in front of his class to talk to the students, with Jaap and Geert, to tell them something about the tour and what we are doing in Delft with DOK, our own public library.

The class was quite surprised when a whole group with Jenny [Levine], Kathryn [Deiss], and our trio entered the room, but jumped to the occasion and came up with great questions. In the end we came up with the idea of spinning the bottle on the university floor with a few students and our group, thus giving our view on the library of the future. Wow, what great material. Fine people with vision, these upcoming librarians of the 21st century. Very hard to say goodbye after only a few hours. But we will meet up with Jenny and Michael in Monterey and play a mean Wii game in the MotherShip.

Jaap preparing for the video
shoot at Dominican University

REARVIEW MIRROR REFLECTIONS:
THE NEW LIBRARIANS OF THE 21ST CENTURY

After a short break for food and coffee in Ann Arbor, in which I took 2 minutes to buy a guitar at the local music shop, we got out on the highway again for a night drive to Chicago.

Still dying from cramps I was hoping to see the next dawn, but had little faith. Still at 1AM we entered the gates at Dominican with our MotherShip, and the security guards were kind enough to let us in to get some sleep on campus ground. It was early morning when we saw Michael Stephens driving up with life-saving drugs.

I have rarely met a man with such a strong positive outlook on library work and the use of technology to help us do a better job. Besides that, he is an excellent teacher and that is reflected in the level of his students.

This man is an example for so many librarians. I have rarely met a man with such a strong positive outlook on library work and the use of technology to help us do a better job. Besides that, he is an excellent teacher and that is reflected in the level of his students. Sharp minds and a healthy thirst for knowledge made for good questions, and we were eager to answer them as good as we could. The group was joined by our precious friends Jenny Levine and Kathryn Deiss, who joined in the debate, and the class really enjoyed this unexpected surprise visit.

The idea of the library without walls, the Bluetooth station with library content that can be hanged everywhere to share information and stories, and the branding and marketing of libraries clearly appealed to the students, and some of them want to come with us to work in our library in Delft for a while. Actually a good idea. We have to work on this exchange-of-students idea as soon as we have some more time.

Before we left we decided to do a little game on the floor of Dominican. Spin the bottle and, if it pointed to you, you had to say something on the future of libraries. As I expected, these students did remarkably well and seem ready for the future. This visit felt so good and gave such an enormous positive boost that my stomach decided not to kill me yet, and we turned south toward the Mortenson Center in Urbana-Champaign, where we were going to meet with Barbara Ford.

MICHAEL STEPHENS' COMMENTARY

There's always excitement when the Shanachies come through town, as their videos and blogging demonstrated, and the campus of Dominican University [www.dom.edu] in River Forest, Illinois, was no exception. My weekend class didn't know what hit them: Erik, Jaap, and Geert demonstrated their website, configured the screens back home at DOK to greet the university from afar, and shared their philosophies of library service. Making stories … telling stories … keeping stories is truly their mantra and one that all of us in the profession should take to heart.

I was proud of the students who joined in the video, sharing their personal take on the future of libraries. In round-robin fashion, each voice came from a unique perspective but still addressed the question: Where will we be in a few years? What will libraries look like? The library concepts and spaces at DOK are a perfect example of this.

Michael Stephens prepares to "spin the library bottle"
during a discussion with his class.

I am also proud, amazed, and awed by what these three story makers, tellers, and keepers accomplished on their journey across our country. I urge students and librarians to look at the edge of our field to see innovation, to look beyond our borders and see globally what's possible in our institutions, and to take on the challenge of creating these spaces and places at home. The inspiration that the Shanachies brought with them will not be forgotten.

Michael Stephens
Assistant Professor
Graduate School of Library and Information Science
Dominican University
River Forest, IL

Jaap, Erik, Michael Stephens, and
Geert pose in front of the MotherShip.

Barbara Ford stands next to the display case of the gifts that associates have brought to Mortenson over the years.

Barbara Ford Connects Librarians Around the World

WEBLOG SHANACHIETOUR

Mortenson Center
for International
Library Programs
Urbana, Illinois
October 20, 2007
9,300 KM traveled

Turning our nose southward we hit the motorway toward Urbana–Champaign and the Mortenson Center, where we have an appointment with Barbara Ford. Barbara has had an amazing career and, as director of the ALA, had the honor to meet President Bill Clinton. She has seen many changes, but definitely sees a great future for libraries.

They are doing a terrific job on cataloging all the new media. That is a big thing in the Netherlands as well. We did some footage (in Dutch) on a Fobid Conference in September in The Hague. Whether it is about gaming or other technology, where Linda Hinchliffe is working in the Undergraduate Library of the Mortenson Center, or about the educa-

The wind was whispering in the yellow leaves as we crawled out of the RV to sing the blues in the desolate landscape of Ohio.

tion of librarians of other countries where it is difficult to have internet access, the Mortenson Center is working on the library future.

It made me realize that the future we are thinking about is so different from the future in other countries. We need to explore and keep our course, but we should never forget and always help those who are behind us. John Wood, did I already say you have our admiration? Your book about creating the Room to Read organization and your good work of building libraries in Third World countries is amazing. We librarians around the globe should work on this. Free access to the web everywhere with reliable, objective information if you want, and good education programs. Wow we have still a lot work ahead of us.

REARVIEW MIRROR REFLECTIONS: NEW LIBRARIANS HAVE TO BE INNOVATIVE AND OPEN-MINDED

The wind was whispering in the yellow leaves as we crawled out of the RV to sing the blues in the desolate landscape of Ohio. This picture was just too good to miss, and we decided to make a recording for the ShanachieTour site. The guitar that we bought in Ann Arbor had an excellent sound and, with an old plough in the background, an improvised windscreen, and a husky voice, we managed to give this day a melancholy start.

After the whirlwind of inspiring ideas in Chicago we did not know what to expect in Urbana–Champaign. Jenny Levine recommended this library, and she went there for her education so they must do a good job here. At first the city seemed impossible to enter as we were not allowed with our RV to go underneath the railway that divides this town. When finally we succeeded to cross over, we suddenly seemed to find ourselves back in Delft, our hometown. There were students everywhere we looked, all dressed in orange and in shirts that had words on them that, even in the Netherlands, would be considered shocking.

After an impressive library career, Barbara Ford is now the head of the Mortenson Center for International Library Programs [www.library.uiuc.edu/mortenson]. It was established by gifts from C. Walter and Gerda B. Mortenson. Its goal is to strengthen international ties among libraries and librarians worldwide for the promotion of peace, education, and understanding. And that is what Barbara does with great passion.

Part of the building where we wanted to go was built underground in the middle of a large square. After a little tour we decided to go for the last light of the day and did the interview with Barbara in our humble MotherShip.

Of course, we were curious to see the differences and similarities that Barbara sees in librarians all over the world. She is very outspoken when it comes to the skills of the librarian of today and of the future. And she is the one who knows. More than 725 librarians from 89 countries follow

Jaap and Erik review the film of the song
they recorded outside one morning.

an education program here. There are great opportunities in working with Web 2.0 and developing new services. "New librarians have to be innovative and non-traditional to meet user needs," she told us. We said amen to that. After this talk, together with our meeting with the students in Chicago, we have stronger faith in a good library future as we leave for the public library of Council Bluffs in Iowa.

BARBARA FORD'S COMMENTARY

Saturday, October 20, 2007, was a busy day at the University of Illinois at Urbana–Champaign. We had a football game (including many people dressed in orange for the event), a modern dance performance in the underground garden of the undergraduate library, and 17 librarians from 14 countries who were at the Mortenson Center in a continuing education program on a visit to an Amish home and farm and the Arthur Public Library. In the midst of this, a large recreational vehicle arrived at the library after overcoming the challenges of driving under the overhead railroad tracks and through the traffic for the various events on campus.

When they finally arrived, it was a real pleasure to talk with the librarians from Delft in the Netherlands about programs at the University

Barbara Ford shares insights during her interview in the MotherShip.

of Illinois at Urbana–Champaign libraries and to hear about the adventures of a cross-country tour of libraries. After their visit I enjoyed watching the Shanachies' progress on the website and learning from their observations.

In December, on my way to an IFLA governing board meeting in The Hague, I visited the Library Concept Center in Delft [where they work] and was very impressed with all that is happening there. The world of libraries is a small one, and the Shanachies' tour provided an opportunity to connect with colleagues who are making a difference and leading libraries into an exciting future. Through sharing experiences and learning from each other we can continue to expand the global reach and local touch of libraries. Onward!

Barbara J. Ford
Director, Mortenson Center for International Library Programs
and Mortenson Distinguished Professor
University of Illinois Library at Urbana–Champaign
Urbana, IL

Council Bluffs entrance

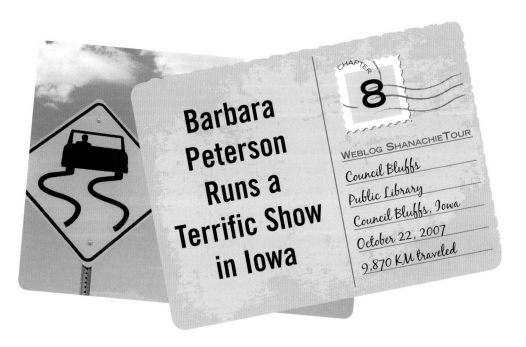

CHAPTER

8

WEBLOG SHANACHIETOUR

Council Bluffs
Public Library
Council Bluffs, Iowa

October 22, 2007

9,870 KM traveled

Barbara Peterson Runs a Terrific Show in Iowa

How big is this country? I feel like there is no end to it. The drone of our rolling MotherShip seems to go on and on. I feel much better and I am so glad with the all the positive reactions on what we are doing. Just goes to show: Think big, librarians, and dream even bigger. If indeed the universe is made of stories, then this ship has only just set sail. I am so proud that we librarians can be the keepers, tellers, and makers of these stories. Come on Melville, help us search for that big white whale.

Well one beauty did catch our attention in Council Bluffs. Worth every mile traveled. What a nice, spacious, clean, and friendly place. The three of us felt right at ease and drank in the atmosphere of this cool public library. We were welcomed by Barbara Peterson, who had us spellbound from the very minute that she started talking. She has a group of great people working there, and Barbara is bright enough to give them ample space to keep them motivated and to come up with good ideas. When your staff takes pleasure and pride in their work and tell it, then you have something special in your hands.

We were impressed with the capability to think beyond the boxes. I mean, getting a percentage of the income of your local casinos and putting that in your library? It is amazing. And it does not stop there. Audiobooks on MP3 players, great movie and music department with an excellent choice and variety. Big compliment there, we were really impressed. Great speakers and lots of events and public debate. Soon they will have their 10-year anniversary. We hope to be invited to their 20th. We will definitely stay in touch. Thanks Barbara. Don't erase or else …

REARVIEW MIRROR REFLECTIONS: MISSION, MISSISSIPPI, MUSIC, MONEY, AND MOTHERSHIP

Council Bluffs Public Library's [www.cbpl.lib.ia.us] Mission Statement is: "The Council Bluffs Public Library exists to inform, enrich and empower every individual in its community, by creating and promoting free and easy access to a vast array of ideas, information and knowledge and by supporting lifelong learning in a welcoming environment."

Most memorable stop being of course the Mississippi River. Great thoughts sprang to mind and turned us into little Mark Twains. What about a library trip way down south, rafting the river with our laptops and studio equipment?

I know … I am a sucker for mission statements. Always have been. More than 400 miles from Urbana and the Mortenson Center, we came to Council Bluffs. Most memorable stop being of course the Mississippi River. Great thoughts sprang to mind and turned us into little Mark Twains. What about a library trip way down South, rafting the river with our laptops and studio equipment? Then it struck me. This river took the life of one of the greatest singers ever. Jeff Buckley (son of Tim) died after a swim in this river in the middle of finishing an album.

A little sad, we stepped into our MotherShip and moved on to the public library of this tidy town in the Midwest. More than 140 years ago this library opened its doors for the first time. It was in 1904 that Andrew Carnegie gave the city $70,000 to build a real library building. The city agreed to spend at least $7,000 yearly for maintenance, which in those days was quite a sum.

Only 10 years ago the library opened a new building that cost $12.5 million, of which 80 percent was paid by the Iowa West Foundation. That is an amazing amount of money, but one look showed us that it was money well-spent. What a beautiful building. Open and spacious. The first thing I saw while we were waiting for Barbara Peterson was the music collection. Besides classical music and jazz music that we found in more libraries, we found an amazing collection of pop music here.

Reaching the Mississippi,
almost halfway across the U.S.

And absolutely up to date. The latest CDs on the charts are stored here upfront. Work of a passionate and inspired music lover for sure.

This library and Barbara listen to their customers and provide them with a good collection with a special interest in new developments such as MP3 players with audiobooks. In order to organize special services, there is always an attempt to bring in money, and marketing is important here. The story of how the three casinos in this town were persuaded to donate a percentage of their income to the library showed us there was no need to worry about this library in Council Bluffs. Barbara knows what she is doing and does it well.

Nebraska was waiting and we had to cross that great empty stretch of flat wild land on our way to Denver and the mountains. Bruce Springsteen was on the radio over the roaring engine of the MotherShip. More than halfway, yet many miles to go. "At the end of every hard earned day we find a reason to believe. ..." [Bruce Springsteen, "Reason to Believe" from the album Nebraska].

BARBARA PETERSON'S COMMENTARY

The phone rang, and on the other end was a voice I did not recognize. It was Erik telling me that "The MotherShip is going to be a little late."

I assured him that was OK and that I would be waiting. As I hung up, I thought, "The MotherShip, what is that?"

Within in the hour we were converged upon by a group of three librarians from the Netherlands. They came in carrying bags, mics, headphones, laptops, and other electronic equipment. My staff said later that they wondered what was going on as the visitors walked through the library to my office. What an interesting experience it was. Erik and his crew talked with me about their project and shared information and video of their library.

Barbara Peterson of the Council Bluffs Public Library

As we walked through the library, people watched and listened to what we were saying. As we went to the A/V area, Erik asked what the Playaways were. I explained that they were audiobooks on an MP3 player and that we checked them out that way. He was fascinated by them. The staff was fascinated by Erik and his crew. We were having so much fun with the interview that the time slipped by in a hurry and suddenly it was time for them to leave. Frankly, I could have talked with them for another hour or so. But, all good things have to come to an end. From here they were traveling to Denver, Colorado.

About a week later, I received an email with a video of the Council Bluffs visit on it. It was very exciting to see what they had put together on the road and in such a short time. This group is definitely talented and inspiring. It was great to talk with library futurists such as Erik and his crew. I hope that that they come back and do a sequel someday, and maybe bring the "FatherShip" this time!

Barbara Peterson
Director
Council Bluffs Public Library
Council Bluffs, Iowa

Michelle Jeske,
Jo Haight
Sarling, and
Crew Treasure
Future History
in Denver

CHAPTER **9**

WEBLOG SHANACHIETOUR

Denver Public Library

Denver, Colorado

October 23, 2007

10,720 KM traveled

It is 6AM. Nebraska alarm. Temperatures are below zero in the Mother-Ship. This to me is Bruce [Springsteen] country. Today we have to cross it to get to Denver, and it turns out to be the big void. A sort of Bermuda Triangle. We lose all contact. No cell phone or internet. Just asphalt and flat emptiness. But I love it. The great hunger for stories is upon us once again so Silver Surfer, my Marvel comic hero, and I ride the highway once again. The great thing is that we pass into another time zone so we gain 1 hour.

Just in time for a delicious lunch with a local bite of tamales, we are welcomed by Diane Lapierre, Michelle Jeske, Laurie [Kubitz-Maness], Jo [Haight Sarling], and other friendly staff members. What a great place. The entrance reminds me a little of an old railway station with beautiful floors and gates to the different departments. We get on board and go back in time with Bruce Hanson, who shows us that they are digitizing the old archives in order to preserve them for the future. This is done with great care and respect and they still maintain the old maps and card system and furniture. There are works of art on the wall that show American history, and the library definitely helps people to know more about where they come from.

Erik and Bruce Hanson talk in the archive room.

In contrast with this form of keeping stories, this library is very modern in the way it shares its stories. Besides the amazing website [denverlibrary.org], it has an online video lending system that we would love to have in Delft. It draws many patrons to the website and is often used. This is best practice indeed. If we as libraries work together and get more rights to more materials to lend out online, we will reach more people. Remember if we don't do it somebody else will. So let's get hold of this part of future library service and work together.

Thanks for everything. We are on our way to Monterey and still enjoying these leftover tamales. For one single moment the hunger is gone and we lay back peacefully in the MotherShip.

REARVIEW MIRROR REFLECTIONS: ARCHIVE OF THE WEST

After the flatness of the Midwest, now we first saw snow on the mountains on the horizon. We had been emailing with Michelle and Diane, and they had promised us lunch with tamales. Never ate them before, but Shanachies are easily tempted with local specialty dishes.

Hungry, we entered the city of Denver. To us, city of the TV series *Dynasty*, home of the Carringtons and wicked Alexis. But this city held a beautiful library. Denver Public Library was opened in 1889 and has a great history. The library now has 23 branches and more than 5 million books. This is impressive. But first, lunch with a group of young librarians, who seemed a little nervous. They clearly did not know what to expect from the Shanachies, and maybe the weeks of travel had taken its toll. We were beginning to look a little like the vagabonds that we are. There was no hiding it anymore.

During our library tour we saw that history was well preserved and very important in this library. There was art on the walls everywhere portraying life in the Old West. There were old city maps and a beautiful room with a sort of tepee and old documents and books. The program of digitization is in full swing in order to make this beautiful stuff available to everyone. There is a great interest in this by the population of Denver, and Bruce Hanson often helps them in their research.

During the tour I was so impressed to hear that 79 percent of the population holds a library card. Wow, in Delft we are proud to have 25

percent with a card. And that is not all. Denver is, of course, so much bigger then Delft, but 10 million items borrowed annually and 450 staff members is big, really big. In the inspiring youth department we sat behind glass in the afternoon sun and Jo Haight Sarling told me about the success of the online videos and how it all began with online audiobooks. But there was so much more. The after-school programs, the Super Saturdays, not-so-rare books and art auctions, Book Lovers Ball, and so on.

During the tour I was so impressed to hear that 79 percent of the population holds a library card.

The Denver Public Library constantly seeks new ways to serve its customers. Therein lies its power. Whether it is the latest bestseller, a video travel guide, or an online collection of historical photographs, there is always something new. That is the Denver Public Library's secret to capturing the imaginations of so many for so long.

We said goodbye to new friends and know that we will meet again in the future. Onwards to Salt Lake City and its architectural wonder, which I think of as "the glass book palace of the north."

MICHELLE JESKE'S COMMENTARY

We ate tamales, they gave us T-shirts, and we were inspired. But not before we had a chance to help Erik, Geert, and Jaap park their large RV in downtown Denver.

We saw them walking up to our building with their shiny silver badges on their cool black T-shirts: LBI, Library Bureau of Investigation. Not exactly the picture of your typical librarians. More a trio of Euro-Techno-Guys. The investigation began with the tamales. It ended with a trip back to the RV to see just how they were living life on the road. In between we talked about Wii, design, music, digital history, art, architecture, privacy, and community. They told us about how their staff designed their beautiful new library. We told them about our work digitizing neighborhood histories. They told us about their cool cell phone customer greetings.

Michelle Jeske, Diane Lapierre,
and Laurie Kubitz-Maness

We told them about our downloadable media service. We shared stories about the challenges of staff keeping up with technology. That's it—the sharing. Learning through conversation. That's what it's about.

As they drove off to a rockin' ranch party in a southern Colorado town, we were left with our own LBI T-shirts and dreams about the ongoing journey of libraries. We may even take a trip of our own.

Michelle Jeske
Manager, Web Information Services and
Community Technology Center
Denver Public Library
Denver, CO

CHAPTER

10

WEBLOG SHANACHIETOUR

John C. Fremont Library
Florence, Colorado
October 24, 2007
11,120 KM traveled

**Kieran Hixon
and Her Brave
Librarians
Throw Away All
Lame Excuses**

**After our admired friend Jenny Levine posted our tour
on her blog,** Kieran Hixon was brave enough to invite the Dutch gang
over to her library. Despite our impossible schedule we really wanted to
visit a small town library to see how it is facing the challenges of the
21st century. Well, did we come to the right place. After an amazing

meal with lots of cows and a good night rest on the ranch, we were ready to see how the 3,500 people of Florence were using their library. And what a lovely library we did find. A real community center with a knitting group, the Wool Gatherers, and a computer class going on as we came in. The night before there had been a lecture on The Day of the Dead, a Mexican celebration.

This library is very much alive. Mostly, as we notice, because of inspired, ambitious, open-minded

This library is very much alive. Mostly, as we notice, because of inspired, ambitious, open-minded staff.

staff. There are never enough budgets or enough hours or whatever reasons you may think of not to go ahead. These people do not count hours or stop because of budget restrictions. They invent ways to do what they want. Game events—why not, the place is packed with teens, who all love the initiative. Changing from a card system to bar codes and a free open source ILS and catalogue for their website, thus saving a lot of money—why not. They were lucky to find Jesse, a 15-year-old wizard, who is implementing all the technology, but then what is luck? We Shanachies believe that if you really want something, you will call upon that sort of luck and it will come to you. Away with the excuses, if they can do it in Florence, you can do it. Let's get on with it. Thank you Kieran and Judy [Van Acker]. Your board can be proud of what you are doing for your community.

On to Salt Lake it is, through the best of scenery. New energy and inspiration. First a meal in the Red Barn and then a night stop in Grand Junction, Colorado. The pictures of Salt Lake look so good. It is almost a pity that we humans need to sleep sometimes.

REARVIEW MIRROR REFLECTIONS: EXPLORING THE WEST

John C. Fremont is known as an explorer of the Western states of the U.S.A. In fact, for a large part of his life, he was sort of illegitimate European American, which he overcame by marriage to a well-to-do American girl by the name of Jessie Benton. Hmm, European and explorer. This was something that we Shanachies needed to learn more about.

We had received a very Web 2.0 invitation from Kieran Hixon. She had read about our coming to America on Jenny Levine's blog (www.the shiftedlibrarian.com) and decided that her library should be included in the tour. "Be proud and tell it" has always been one of our slogans so we could not ignore this. And we were glad that we went over.

First a very hospitable welcome with great food, then late-night guitar playing and storytelling, and then a good night's sleep on the ranch. Next morning I had to ride a horse and try to be a cowboy chasing wild mountain lions.

But there was not enough time. We had to go to their library to see their Koha ILS, which had been downloaded, implemented, and tweaked by Jesse, a teenage library fan. Amazing what a few passionate people with a small budget can do. They probably work around the clock, but they showed us that you do not have to be big and over-staffed or whatever to do all the hot new library stuff. They have game nights, computer clubs, summer reading, and so on. Check out the website [www.florenceco library.org] and be amazed. Links to podcasts, test preparations for driving

Judy Van Acker, Erik, and their friend Lovey on the ranch

Dillon Pinnacles, Blue Mesa Reservoir, Colorado

licenses, library blogs, web tools, but also local links, special teens web space, it goes on and on.

As far as making the most of little time and budget, this library stands alone. We bowed our heads in admiration, and in silence we walked back to the MotherShip. There are still many times that we go back in our heads to the wonderful 2 days in Colorado. Thanks super librarians; the world awaits …

KIERAN HIXON AND JUDY VAN ACKER'S COMMENTARY

It was early evening when an RV half the size of our library pulled into the parking lot. Three abreast, they strode across the street with matching Shanachie shirts, like men on a mission. We all sat at a big table while they hit our Wi-Fi. We chatted for awhile, but could see that they were beat.

They got back into their MotherShip and headed out to the ranch. Grilled steaks, beer, and guitar brought conversations. Jaap streamed video of the DOK library, opening our world to what libraries can be. We saw the vision, we saw the potential—culture, music, books—in a library —vibrant and possible. The Dutch guys seemed honestly interested in

our little rural library. What impressed us the most was their passion and their drive—for God's sake, it was literally across the country! It inspired us. And then we began thinking too ...

P.S. We would really like to re-record our song for you—we are better now, we swear!

Kieran Hixon
Tech Services
John C. Fremont Library District
Florence, CO

Judy Van Acker
S.E. Regional Library Consultant
Colorado Library Consortium
Florence, CO

Kieran Hixon, Judy, and Erik playing guitar

CHAPTER **11**

WEBLOG SHANACHIETOUR

Salt Lake City
Public Library
Salt Lake City, Utah
October 25, 2007
11,570 KM traveled

Let Andrew Shaw's Northern Star Library Be a Guide

Coming toward Salt Lake, we are a bit disappointed at first. After a drive through beautiful scenery, we see enormous smog hanging over downtown Salt Lake. We expected a clean, healthy town, but as Andrew [Shaw], our tour guide, explains, it is because the mountains hold the air. A light breeze and it's gone.

*The glass elevators are part of
this library's "transparency."*

The disappointment had already made way for amazement and admiration. Wow, what architecture. The sun on all those windows. All that light. The vision of transparency is proving to be such a success. This is how libraries should be.

Even the elevators are all glass. There are but few things kept behind closed doors. You can see that the patrons love it. It is their library, their bookshelves, their computers, their music, their magazines. So why should they not get a good look at their stuff? When the people in the library, both staff and visitors, take pride in the library there is room to grow. To really become something special.

We have to work on that pride and go around and tell it to anyone who wants to listen. We have the best job in the world. It may be easier to realize that when you are standing in a garden on top of a beautiful building, but it is true, and let that building be an example. Let's share ideas. I mean, a department of independent magazines, mostly privately made by patrons and only one copy, donated to the library. Hundreds of them in all colors and shapes. This is Shanachie style to the limit. We love it.

*Some of Salt Lake City Public
Library's stunning architecture*

But there is much more. Everywhere there are surprises in the building. Hidden quotations, little rooms in the youth department where kids find refuge to read quietly or game online. Art exhibitions with original drawings of The Simpsons. A coffee corner. It does not stop. Another great thing was the cooperation with the shops in the building. They even have a library bookstore and a place where people can go if they want help in their writing. A sort of writing class that can help to get people's writings published. I hope our video may inspire librarians to make the trip to Salt Lake. You have to see it for yourself. The library without walls is getting close here. No censorship, open on Sundays, and that in the Mormon capital of the world.

We have to leave. Head south for that devil's pit Las Vegas, but not before we inhale some fresh air in Bryce.

REARVIEW MIRROR REFLECTIONS: THE CITY'S LIBRARY

"A dynamic civic resource that promotes free and open access to information, materials and services to all members of the community to advance knowledge, foster creativity, encourage the exchange of ideas, build community and enhance the quality of life."

This is what first springs up when opening the website [www.slcpl.org]. A message so strong on such a prominent place means vision and strong will to reach out to the public. An openness that we find back in the architecture. This glass building is carefully designed and shows the high value and aspiration this city has for its library. The six-story curving wall embraces the public plaza, with shops and services at ground level, reading galleries above, and a 300-seat auditorium. Especially the shops with related articles, like books and office equipment, posters, and comics, give this building added value. There is even a writer's help desk/shop. People who write poetry or prose can come in and get help when they are stuck. They are also given advice on how to get published or can enter competitions.

The garden on the roof is amazing and gives a 360-degree view of Salt Lake and the mountains. But it does not stop there. The spiralling fireplaces on four floors, the beautiful youth department with moveable, translucent curtains or clouds may be pulled across the space to provide shade when necessary. There is an alcove filled with multimedia equipment loaded with educational games and learning programs. There are two special spaces tucked under the reflecting pool of the plaza.

Designed to free a child's imagination, these rooms are places for dreaming, playing, reading, and inventing. During the summer months, children can enjoy the adjacent terrace where gently flowing waterfalls cascade down the walls and enjoy storytelling in the open air.

Designed to free a child's imagination, these rooms are places for dreaming, playing, reading, and inventing.

Everywhere in the library there are hidden quotations that surprise you, and the light is always different. There is a special room for the teens near the cafeteria that is called the Canteena with special magazines and materials that they find interesting. There is a collection of DVDs and CDs; there is a technology center and training lab that offers 42 computer stations with internet access. These computers have been partially provided through a Gates grant. Staff is trained and available to assist users as they write papers, work on resumes, and develop computer skills.

We were impressed by the art department and especially charmed with the 'zines: a whole collection of magazines made by people in often only one or two copies. Andrew Shaw, who guided us through this magnificent building, was so inspiring and motivated that he confirmed our hope that there is a large group of librarians out there who get it. Librarians who know what to do to meet the challenges that face us. With this in mind, we set out for Vegas and the Californian coastline. We were ready to face ancient nature and the exiting future of libraries.

ANDREW SHAW'S COMMENTARY

The Salt Lake City Public Library draws in new visitors every day, and giving tours always provides a fresh lens through which I can view our library.

Despite having driven most of the way across the country, Erik, Jaap, and Geert brought energy and a child-like awe with them. Showing them our building's many great features (from the roof garden to the art gallery, the Urban Room to the "attic" playroom in the Children's Library) and watching their eyes light up reminded me, once again, of the magical place where I work every day.

Jaap with Tania Toro, Erik, and
Andrew Shaw at the desk in Salt Lake

But taking librarians through The City Library, especially those who are as interested in community-building and storytelling as the Shanachie crew, is an extra treat. Although The City Library has built a grand building, the real impressive part is how it reflects the foundational ideas: the transparency, the community, the discovery, the drive for excellence, and the view of the future. Being able to share these ideals with the Shanachie crew who, in turn, shared them with so many others, seems like the ultimate act of the public library—sharing information and ideas, and passing them on to the wider community.

Thank you for the opportunity to be part of the ShanachieTour. At the end of the segment on The City Library, Erik said he would be back. I certainly hope it's true!

Andrew Shaw
Assistant Manager of Community Affairs
Salt Lake City Public Library
Salt Lake City, Utah

ShanachieTour

Scenery from
Yosemite National Park

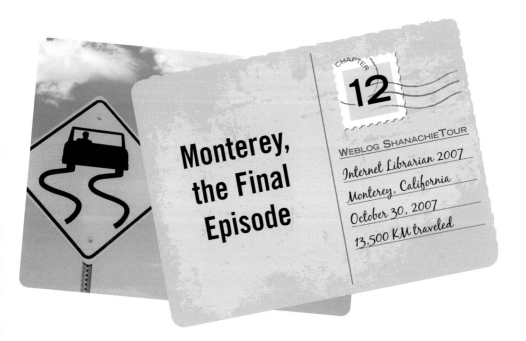

CHAPTER

12

WEBLOG SHANACHIETOUR

Internet Librarian 2007

Monterey, California

October 30, 2007

13,500 KM traveled

Monterey, the Final Episode

There it is. After almost 9,000 miles, including flight distance, we are guided by the sound of the sea lions towards our hotel and the conference center. Right next to Fisherman's Wharf we park the Mother-Ship to leave her behind for 2 nights. We have been lost in beautiful national parks without internet, so there is a lot of work to be done before we are ready for the presentation. And there are so many friendly people to talk to. Jane Dysart, Sarah [Houghton-Jan], Aaron [Schmidt], Michael [Stephens], Jenny [Levine], Kathy [Dempsey], and of course Dick Kaser, the man who invited us over here. All inspiring people and every time we leave our editing room we meet new people.

This project has been such a wonderful way of exchanging ideas and making people proud of their library and to be a librarian. But as I said, there was work to be done and I was getting more nervous by the minute. Jaap suggested doing the last edition of the ShanachieTour live with the audience. Brilliant, but that would mean that he and Geert would be busy filming and thus leaving me to do the presentation. The whole afternoon people came up asking for the time that we would be on and it was obvious there would be quite a crowd. That there would be near

For the last segment of the movie, Jaap and Geert record Erik and the audience live during their Internet Librarian presentation.

to 700 librarians and that we would start off with an earthquake 5.6 on the Richter scale was not expected.

Edo [our Dutch colleague who had joined us for the Monterey presentation] impressed the crowd with the Bluetooth push service that sent out the [animated] Shanachie trailer to the mobile phones. Then we threw in our boss, showing a short video tour around our own library DOK. After that, Jaap turned on the camera and I invited the crowd to be part of the tour film and they went wild. From then on, the presentation could not go wrong.

Is this the end or the start of the beginning?

Such a nice crowd. Good answers to the questions. Sincere interest in the stories. Shanachie highlight for sure. After a standing ovation, we took 5 minutes in the hotel to finish that bottle of bubbles and then into the night to enjoy every minute in the company of new and old friends.

Is this the end or the start of the beginning? The ShanachieTour will never end; we are already on our way to new stories and new horizons. Hope to see you all soon on one of our stops. And please Dick, take good care of that guitar. We may sing a couple of songs in April at CIL.

Before leaving Monterey, the Shanachies gave their U.S. tour guitar to Information Today, Inc.'s VP of Content, Dick Kaser, who had

REARVIEW MIRROR REFLECTIONS:
THE ROAD TO INTERNET LIBRARIAN

Salt Lake City Public Library was the last library on our list—well, we had more, but that would have been impossible. I guess we have to come back. That is, if you will have us. But the reception everywhere has been so warm and the people so friendly that I put my faith in that. Rather than in Vegas, which was our little detour on our way to Monterey. Passing through and staying overnight in the wonders of nature—Bryce Canyon, Zion, Death Valley, Yosemite, it was unbelievable. Warning signs for bears made our childhood books come to life. We were living the story.

Then Las Vegas, what can I say. This town did not work for me. Although I immediately realized that you cannot say that after 1 night, without a proper guide. It was just so much. All the temptations designed to make

Erik and Jaap filming in Bryce Canyon

you spend your money. Too many choices. Maybe a bit like the internet. Such a wide wide world web. To use it effectively, if that's what you want, it is handy to have a guide. And we librarians can be that guide. We can and must be out there as a good reliable friend. Just as much as inside the building, we need to inspire and stimulate and maybe, as Paul Holdengräber puts it, irritate.

We picked up Edo Postma in Vegas. Together with DOK, our library, Edo (who works for ProBiblio, a Dutch library association) had done a lot of innovative research and was at that moment working on new tools with regard to mobile phones. He brought a mysterious piece of machinery with him that he would be showing at the conference.

Well, I was tired of all these mountains. I wanted the ocean. I wanted to see my friends in Monterey. At this point it was just a few hours before I could take that dive. I couldn't wait.

After inhaling the fresh sea air and having the time of our lives in Monterey, we headed to San Francisco to say goodbye to our beloved MotherShip and fly back to Amsterdam with our suitcases full of passion for libraries and great hope for their future.

KATHY DEMPSEY'S COMMENTARY

I first met the Shanachies at the end of their trek in Monterey at the Internet Librarian conference. As an editor for Information Today, Inc., I often go to the company's shows, not only to cover them for my publications, but also to work at the exhibit booth, blog, and meet with colleagues.

On the eve of this conference, my boss Dick Kaser had planned to take several of us editors out for an informal dinner meeting. He told us he'd also invited "the Dutch guys," some men that he'd gotten onto the program to speak at the show's annual Evening Session. I'd already noticed their foreign names on the advance program—having been to Holland several times myself, anything with a "van de" jumps out at me. Weeks earlier, I'd made a mental note to try to meet these men at the show so I could chat about the country that I'd come to love vacationing in. Little did I know what fate had in store.

My job had kept me way too busy to read blogs, and I didn't even realize until I was heading to Monterey that this trio had been on a cross-country trek for weeks, meeting and interviewing librarians across America. I knew only that Dutch people were cool, and that I wanted to check them out.

So that Sunday evening, familiar faces appeared at our hotel lobby meeting point one by one. But we were still waiting for our Dutch speakers. Suddenly there they were, four Euro-looking guys dressed in black, shaking hands all around. Straight away our group walked out into the balmy California night, chatting our way toward a seafood dinner on the Old Fisherman's Wharf.

That evening would re-invigorate my life.

It didn't take long for me to become fascinated by Erik Boekesteijn, Jaap van de Geer, Geert van den Boogaard, and Edo Postma. First of all, I'm a sucker for a good European accent, so they had me at "Hello." Second, they had an amazing story to tell about their road trip. And finally, they were so charming and thoughtful. They were even patient as I practiced pronouncing their names and weaved my limited Dutch vocabulary into conversation. What was not to like?

Edo Postma (standing) and the Shanachies showed off their beloved MotherShip after dinner.

I also had a tremendous professional curiosity about this gang and their work. As the long-time editor of the *Marketing Library Services* newsletter, I've seen and heard about tons of different library publicity projects. But this one was like none before. Yes, others have interviewed librarians about the future, but somehow the Shanachies were different. I think it was because they were seeing American libraries through the eyes of outsiders, filtering the info through their own lenses, and reflecting it back to us in a way that let us see ourselves in a whole different light. These guys, I soon realized, were really on to something.

After a couple of hours of wonderful food and conversation, we started back toward the hotel, and they invited us to come see the big RV they'd been living in during their trek. I was too curious to decline. Dick and I walked with them to check it out, had some more laughs, and took some more pictures. Back at the hotel, I shared an elevator with them, and as I stepped out, bidding them all goodnight, I was still captivated.

Over the course of the conference, I spent more time with them, learned about their own library, and was amazed at some of the innovations there. I made sure I got a front-row seat for their Tuesday evening presentation, proudly wearing the LBI ShanachieTour T-shirt they'd given me. When that was over and they were mobbed by new fans, I felt myself being pulled into the phenomenon. People were trying to write down their URL so they could go back and read their travel blog. Of course, nobody knew how to spell "Shanachie," but since it was emblazoned across my shirt, I started helping people. Thinking I knew all about the trip, attendees began asking me questions too. I felt as if I were part of it. I had become part of it. Seeing all the excitement surrounding this project only fueled my own interest, and soon I became a full-fledged Shanachie Evangelist. I decided that I had to help spread the word about their view of libraries, their great documentary film, and their spirit that was so contagious and invigorating.

Seeing all the excitement surrounding this project only fueled my own interest, and soon I became a full-fledged Shanachie Evangelist.

—Kathy Dempsey

The next day, before we all hugged goodbye as they left Monterey, we'd already made plans to keep in touch. And we all kept those promises. First via email, then again in person at the Computers in Libraries (CIL) conference in April 2008, I've had the pleasure of forming individual relationships with each of the three Shanachies, who are so talented in

their own ways. Geert, the tour's mic-man and wonderful photographer, has explained some of his work as an industrial design consultant, which I find both visionary and fascinating. Jaap, the video genius, has won my deep admiration for his constant hunger for—and quick mastery of—new technologies. And Erik, the consummate frontman, has constantly amazed me with his way with words, especially since English is not even his first language. And all of them share such a sense of wonder and curiosity, a thirst for life, and an unending determination. ... Did I mention that I've become an evangelist?

And now that you've read their tale, have you?

Kathy Dempsey
Editor, Marketing Library Services
and consultant, Libraries Are Essential
Medford, NJ

Afterword

Now, in 2008, looking back on this amazing trip last fall, we realize that the smoke is still clearing. When we were at Michael Stephens' apartment almost a year ago for the making of the documentary "If You're Not Gaming, You're Losing," we came up with the idea for this road trip. Only a month later, we found sponsors and were able to draw up the plan and to approach the libraries we wanted to visit.

Of course, we totally believed in the value of a trip like this, with regard to the exchange of best-practice ideas of libraries in the U.S.A. and bringing these ideas to the Internet Librarian conference in Monterey, but the warmth and passion and true belief in the library of the future that we encountered was something beyond our expectations. Especially in times when the function of the library is under debate and the book circulation is decreasing, the necessity of this Shanachie work is evident.

About the Authors

Erik Boekesteijn works in the Communication and Innovation Department at DOK, the library concept center in Delft, the Netherlands. His work includes marketing, promotion, and innovation. Together with Jaap van de Geer, he works on many DOK studio productions. They are also hired as a team by other libraries for a period of time to reorganize their library. Erik is one of the founders of the UGame ULearn project, which promotes gaming in libraries on a national and international level. He has a degree in English and is specialized in the area of interpreter/translator. He has written articles for *Computers in Libraries* and *Marketing Library Services*.

San Francisco:
the end of the line

Jaap van de Geer is head of the IT department of DOK. He is responsible for the self-invented unique ILS called ClienTrix, which recently integrated Google Book Search. He has a Library Science Degree with a specialization on IT. Jaap works on the website of DOK and is cameraman and editor on many productions of the DOK Studio department. He is also responsible for the important gaming project, UGame ULearn. Jaap wrote an article about new media for *Bibliotheekblad*, the Dutch equivalent of *Library Journal*, and co-founded the first Dutch weblog on libraries and librarianship, OBLOG.

Geert van den Boogaard is responsible for acquisition and external funding at DOK. He has an M.Sc. in Industrial Design and has his own Design and Advice bureau, BOOG. In addition to fundraising, he works on signage and many other projects for DOK including Agora, the Story Board of Your Life project. He is an avid amateur photographer.